Kay Brown

GILEAD
BOOKS
PUBLISHING

Gilead Books Publishing
Corner Farm
West Knapton
Malton
North Yorkshire YO17 8JB UK
www.GileadBooksPublishing.com

First published in Great Britain, October 2015
2 4 6 8 10 9 7 5 3 1

British Library Cataloguing-in-Publication Data:
A catalogue record for this book is available from the British Library.

ISBN: 978-0-9932090-1-7

The publisher makes every effort to ensure that the papers used in our books are made from trees that have been legally sourced from well-managed and credibly certified forests by using a printer awarded FSC & PEFC chain of custody certification.

Cover design: Nathan Ward
Illustrations: ©Anna Tash

Contents

Foreword

In today's modern world we love to know the detail about people's lives. Reality shows abound, some not so good, but some very interesting ones, which give us an insight into the life behind the image.

When we read of people encountering Jesus we marvel at their stories, but Kay opens the stories up for us even more, gives us a measured insight into the lives of the people who met Jesus—the situations they were facing, the thoughts that might have been running through their minds and, of course, the transformation that emerged from those special meetings with Jesus.

Not only does Kay lead us into more detail of people's lives and help us to understand the stories more fully, she then touches our own lives with words of prayer that open up our own minds and imaginations—and possible transformation by the Lord in our lives too?

In our all-too-busy lives, take time out to enjoy these reflections and the blessings they bring. Thank you Kay, for sharing them with us.

Rev Robert S.T. Allan LLB DipLP BD
Falkirk Trinity Church

Preface

Then they came to Jericho. As Jesus and his disciples, together with a large crowd, were leaving the city, a blind man, Bartimaeus (that is son of Timaeus), was sitting by the roadside begging. When he heard that it was Jesus of Nazareth, he began to shout all the more, "Son of David, have mercy on me."
Many rebuked him and told him to be quiet, but he shouted all the more, "Son of David, have mercy on me!"
Jesus stopped and said, "Call him." So they called to the blind man, "Cheer up! On your feet! He's calling you."
Throwing his cloak aside, he jumped to his feet and came to Jesus.
"What do you want me to do for you?" Jesus asked him.
The blind man said "Rabbi, I want to see."
"Go," said Jesus, "your faith has healed you."
Immediately he received his sight and followed Jesus along the road. Mark 10: 46-52

Now I See has been both a challenge and a tremendous privilege to write. From Blind Bartimaeus, who receives more than he dared hope for at the hands of Jesus, to the ten lepers healed at the sound of Jesus' voice.

Nicodaemus who meets Jesus at night and in so doing is touched in his soul by 'seeing' that Jesus is both the Law and the Prophets. The woman with the issue of blood who dares to do the unthinkable and touch Jesus' garment is given the amazing gift of seeing her true worth.

Our hearts are moved at the plight of Jairus as he begs Jesus to heal his daughter and then sees a miracle!

We meet the woman bent double and share in her joy as she sees the faces of her neighbours instead of only their feet and finds herself reinstated as a Daughter of Abraham.

A man bed ridden and useless is lowered through the roof by his friends to Jesus feet. He is healed in body, mind and spirit and 'sees' the wonder of who Jesus is.

Then we meet Zacchaeus! A wee man with a big problem—money! That is, until he comes face to face with Jesus and he 'sees' where his true wealth lies.

Little did I imagine when I tentatively wrote *Come See This Man* that it would be followed by *Born For You*, and *Now I See.*

Whilst writing *Now I See* I have been on a journey of listening and praying resulting in a fresh awareness of how the people who were healed by Jesus might have felt; not only felt, but were gloriously enabled to ‘see’ the truth of their worth in God.

May you 'see' and encounter the healing, restoring love of God as you read and like Bartimaeus not only 'see' but follow Jesus along the road of life.

Lord, open our eyes to see and open our hearts to love.

Many Blessings,

Kay

Acknowledgments

Thank you from my heart to all my friends, who have so generously encouraged me to write this third book *Now I See*. A special thank you to those of you, who, having read, *Come See This Man* and *Born For You* have asked for more. Writing in this way is a very humbling experience and would not be possible without the support and prayers of family, church family and friends.

I am so grateful to Chris at Gilead for his constant support and willingness to publish yet a third book and also to Anna for her beautifully simple illustrations.

I am truly indebted to Rev Iain Goring, Neil McLennan and Pauline McAuslan for taking the time in their busy lives to read *Now I See* and for commenting in such perceptive ways. My grateful thanks to you all.

A big thank you to the Rev Robert Allan, for giving so generously of himself in writing the Foreword. Knowing how busy he is I am truly appreciative of his gift of time and talents in commenting in such an insightful way.

My continuing thanks to my husband John for his support in editing and his constant support with the computer.

I give grateful thanks to God for his enabling, gracious presence, for without Him none of this would be possible.

Thank You and God Bless You All.

Blind Bartimaeus

Then they came to Jericho. As Jesus and his disciples, together with a large crowd, were leaving the city, a blind man, Bartimaeus (that is Son of Timaeus), was sitting by the roadside begging. When he heard that it was Jesus of Nazareth, he began to shout, "Jesus Son of David, have mercy on me."
Many rebuked him and told him to be quiet, but he shouted all the more, "Son of David, have mercy on me!"
Mark 10:46-52

The heat, the heat, it's burning into every part of me and I can't do a thing about it. I'm here until sunset. I know that only too well. But I've got to eat. And, being blind, I'm forced to beg or I starve. Sometimes people are generous, so I eat. But, often they spit at me and shout that I must be guilty of some dreadful sin! Then there is the noise and the smell to tolerate; overpowering my being. It's as if being blind highlights sounds and smells, making them more intense.

Blind! Blind! Blind! Why, oh why, Lord do you allow me to be blind? Don't you understand that being blind makes me feel less than human? No, it's more than that. I feel robbed of being a man—a man able to work, to be head of a family, to hold a position in the town. And all of these things are denied me because I'm blind!

Lord! Lord! Lord! I sometimes feel blinded in my very soul. I have lost all hope of being accepted as a man; as a descendent of Abraham. There is only mockery and contempt from all the neighbours about my blindness. Do you hear me Lord? I'm blind!

This constant struggle to draw breath and to have to beg for money to be able to eat. It's like being in bondage—held by the chains of blindness. No, not only blindness, but poverty and misery and the cold creeping fear of isolation, bringing with it the awful sense that I've been abandoned; abandoned by you Lord! Abandoned by the God of Abraham, Isaac and Jacob. Well, that's certainly something to think about, especially as we are not even supposed to utter your name, because you are so holy.

Holy! Huh! How can you, a holy God, allow me to suffer in this way? Well, there is one thing for sure, I may be blind, but I am able to think, to reason. And, you have given me a voice worthy of a man. Do you not hear me roaring at you about how I feel? No self respecting man should have to feel this way. But then, of course, men are not supposed to show they have feelings. Jeremiah and Isaiah suffered and felt and they were great prophets and men. So, maybe, *me* telling *YOU* how I feel is fine.

This heat! This heat! It's almost too much to bear today. And that's strange, because I usually cope with the heat. Today is different. I feel as if my entire body is being held in the grip of some kind of tomb of penetrating darkness. It's sapping my strength.

What's that? What are *they* all talking about? Somebody called Jesus?

I've been so busy telling you what I think and feel, that I've missed what's being said by the crowds. And more important, there's nothing in my begging bowl. Now see what you've caused to happen! I'm not only blind, but penniless, after an entire morning out here in this heat! This blackness is just too much. I might as well die and then the blindness wouldn't matter because there would only be blackness anyway.

Now I remember! It's been rumoured that this man, Jesus, is coming to Jericho. And everyone—well it seems like everyone—has gone crazy about him. They're all talking about this Jesus. Apparently he comes from Nazareth of all places! They're saying that he has a wonderful ability to explain the things of God, in a way that helps people see and understand the truth for themselves.

Huh! What use is that to a blind man? I don't want to see the truth in my head—whatever that might mean. That's all right for everyone else. I just want to see with my eyes.

Mind you, it's said he is a healer as well. So what? What's he going to do for a man like me? I'll never be noticed at the side of the road, surrounded by a crowd this size. Anyway, listening to all the talk around me, it's obvious I'm considered too ragged and stinking to be given a sight of this Jesus.

There I go again; sight, seeing, understanding! Absolute rubbish! There's only hopeless despair in my being and a blackness that fills my head and grabs my eyes in a fierce grip of nothingness. No, I daren't cry! Men just don't! To cry would be to lose the last vestige of being a son of Abraham. And that's all I imagine I have left.

This noise is beyond endurance today. And it's all because they are still shouting about this man Jesus. They're saying that he is going into Jericho. So he has to pass this way. He's coming along this road. Maybe, if I could just push forward a little, I might be able to see him. There I go again, see him! I must be losing all sense of reason. If I could just get through this barrier of legs in front of me, I would be nearer the side of the road. Just a little more; and I'll be there.

Now what? I stink. I'm in rags. I can't even see. So how am I ever going to find out about this Jesus? I could use my voice and call out, even roar like I do at you Lord. But, that would be so demeaning. Everyone would laugh and shout at me. They might even spit or push me away. No, I will just have to wait in silence.

Silence, what do I mean by silence? I don't really know, because my soul is in constant conflict with you, Lord. I discuss my anger, my resentment, and my fears with you constantly. And, you never answer me. Do you?

I'm missing something here. There is a stillness. A calm. A silence. No-one is speaking. And yet there is noise everywhere. It's this tomb I'm in. But it is different. Hope is flickering like a tiny flame in the black depths. A warmth is spreading all over me like a living flame expelling all the hopelessness, fear, misery and abandonment. The warmth becomes a searing white flame pervading my being and penetrating my fear of derision.

Then it happens. He is right there in front of me. The power of his love overwhelms me and I roar out with all my being, "Jesus, Son of David, have mercy on me!" Of course, they all tell me to be quiet. But, His presence enfolds me with a power I have never known before. I know no fear in His wonderful presence. So, I call out again, "Jesus Son of David, have mercy on me!"

Astonished, I hear Jesus say, "Call him." Then the miracle happened—the crowd, who were so against me, encourage me forward. And, as I stumble to my feet I hear him ask me, "What do you want me to do for you?"

I utter the words, "Rabbi I want to see."

"Go", said Jesus, "your faith has made you whole."

My heart swells within me and my very soul responds. Lord, you have heard my voice! The light of his presence sears my eyes, and the fierce grip of nothingness and blackness are gone.

There is only *him*.

As *he* looks at me and *I* look at *him*, I see the God of Abraham, Isaac and Jacob—the God of all eternity. I can see! I am made whole!

> Where we are blind, Father help us to see.
>
> Open our eyes to see you.
>
> Open our hearts to love you.
>
> Open our souls to receive you.
>
> Open our entire being to seeing your glory in the lives you have given us.

Daughter of Abraham

Then should not this woman, a daughter of Abraham, whom Satan has kept bound for eighteen long years be set free on the Sabbath day from what bound her?

Luke 13: 10-17

I'm healed! Healed!

I can't take it in! This whole experience is beyond my wildest imaginings. It's so wonderful to see the faces of all my neighbours and friends. And being able to look at the colour of their eyes and hair is a special gift. As for being able to reach out and clasp their hands properly—that makes me feel really human again.

Oh! Thank you, thank you Lord for setting me free, free to lift my face to the sun and the sky. I almost ache with delight at being able to see such a breathtakingly, beautiful sight. Ache! I can't believe that an ache could be so wonderful. I've never ached with joy before. This ache is so different from the ache of body and soul I've suffered for so long.

Eighteen years bent double, my back in constant pain, my neck creaking and groaning like the rope on the water bucket, and my hands often blistered from clutching my stick; the stick that has kept me from falling onto my face as I struggled to walk to the well each day.

God has certainly blessed me with good neighbours, who have always carried my water jar for me. Now I can carry it myself.

I won't need my stick. I'll even be able to sit on the wall and speak to my friends face to face. No more struggling to see them. No more feeling isolated from others, because I couldn't look at them. I could only ever see their feet and sometimes, on a good day, their knees.

Jesus has lifted me from the pit of pain and despair and he has, in the words of the Psalm, 'healed all my diseases.'

It's even more than that. When he touched me, strength flowed into every part of my being like a mighty rushing wind. A touch like water, wind and fire—all of it roaring through me healing me, body and soul.

No more pain. No more fear. No more dreading each day of pain. But, most amazing of all, I feel clean. Clean. Clean to the tips of my toes. Even my sins are forgiven.

I am redeemed. This knowledge of redemption is even more precious than my physical release. I no longer feel bitter, angry or resentful, and my fierce anger at God has gone. In its place there is the most enveloping peace I have ever known.

As that peace penetrates my whole being I am aware that Jesus is no ordinary man. He has to have come from God. Could Jesus possibly be the Messiah?

Now it starts—the complaints and accusations being thrown at Jesus by the rulers of the Synagogue. Their anger is so tangible that I feel as if I'm trapped by it and their desire to control Jesus. I can't lose my redemption and healing, I just can't!

My heart feels as if it's being squeezed and squeezed, like we squeeze an orange to get the juice out. And then, of course, there's nothing much left of the fruit; only the shredded flesh.

Oh! Maybe I shouldn't have come, because then I wouldn't have missed my freedom. I would just have put up with being disabled and all the restrictions that being bent over inflicted on me. Always staring at the ground—only seeing the dust and stones under my feet. My feet! I know every ridge and mark on my toes, I even recognise the feet of my friends before they speak. Strange how even feet are all different, even unique.

"There are six days for work. So come and be healed on those days not the Sabbath." He can't be serious! Jesus has just healed, yes really healed me; not only physically but spiritually as well. And all this Pharisee can do is rant and rave about it being the Sabbath.

It's as if he's jealous of Jesus and needs to exert control over, not only him, but all of us! This man's thinking is so empty and devoid of any love. No wonder my heart feels as if the very life is being wrung out of it.

No! I will not allow this Pharisee to steal this wonderful gift of healing and wholeness away from me—Sabbath or no Sabbath.

"You hypocrites! Doesn't each of you on the Sabbath untie his ox or donkey from the stall and lead it out to give it water?"

At the sound of Jesus' voice my heart fills with an overwhelming joy and I feel a confidence from him flowing in to my being. And at the same time an amazing knowledge; yes, it is a knowledge. An absolute knowledge of Jesus' authority penetrates my mind. I feel as if I've been given a glimpse of Almighty God himself.

He's really putting the Pharisees in their place. And, what he's saying to them about the Sabbath is so pointedly true that all the people are laughing and nodding and agreeing with him. His teaching is illuminating, freeing, bringing an extra depth to my healing. He's healing my soul. It looks as if he's healing all my friends and neighbours as well—in their minds, wills and emotions. We're all being given a new freedom of understanding of God's love and care.

There it is again—a mighty rushing wind filling my breath. It's as if I'm being filled with *him.* The fire of his spirit envelops my heart with a searing love which threatens to overpower me. An amazing sense of Jesus' purity strikes at my soul and I am clean. Yes! Really clean, for the first time in my life. Jesus has healed more than my body.

His gift of healing is his forgiveness, releasing my heart to love.

His gift of healing is his love, poured into me.

His gift of healing is his grace, shared in his touch.

His gift of healing is his light of truth, shining into my soul.

His gift of healing is the knowledge that Jesus is Lord! Yes Lord!

The crowning glory of all this healing is held like a precious jewel in his next words, "Then should not this woman, a daughter of Abraham, whom Satan has kept bound for eighteen long years, be set free on the Sabbath day from what bound her?"

My heart is soaring towards a life beyond anything I have ever known before. No one, not even the

Pharisees can rob me now. Jesus is the giver of my new life.

He is the wind, the water and the fire; the very Spirit of God himself; the very God of Abraham. And, I am his daughter.

> Lord, when we are bowed down by life's difficulties and are in need of your healing, release our souls with your forgiveness.
>
> Lord, when we feel unloved pour the warmth of your love into our beings.
>
> Lord, when we are angry or afraid anoint our feelings with your grace.
>
> Lord, when we struggle in the darkness of doubt pour your light of truth into our souls.
>
> Lord, when we imagine we are all alone, envelop us with your presence.
>
> May we be moved to cry out, "Jesus is Lord!"

Four Friends

He said to the paralysed man, "I tell you, get up, take your mat and go home." Immediately he stood up in front of them, took what he had been lying on and went home praising God. Luke 5:24b-25

My friends are determined to take me to see this new preacher, teacher, healer or whatever he is! I'm really not sure about going. After all, I can't walk. In fact if I'm honest with myself I can hardly even sit up on my own.

The constant tiredness overcomes me until I am not even able to think, it's like being paralysed in my thinking never mind in my legs. I'm useless. Altogether useless.

I'm useless as a man, useless to my family, useless as a member of the village. I'm even useless in my faith as a good Jew. I am not able go to worship in the Synagogue so the Priests and Pharisees all consider me to be a useless sinner. I can't pay for sacrifices and I've certainly no money to pay for the tithes and offerings expected of me.

Useless. Again. And again. And again.

So, what on earth can a travelling preacher and teacher do for me—a useless cripple?

My friends have done nothing but talk about him day after day. Of course they've been to hear him speak and are adamant that he has healed the sick and even given sight to the blind. I really don't believe their stories. It's just not possible that an ordinary man could be capable of healing. After all not even the Priests or the Pharisees have ever healed anyone—at least not to my knowledge.

They're a swollen headed lot, these Priests and Pharisees. Huh! They certainly don't know what it's like to feel helpless. They are all so busy using the Law to make us ordinary mortals, not only feel useless, but believe that we are useless. And worse still, that we're even without hope.

The whole idea of taking me to see this Jesus is useless. How will they get me there in the first place? Anyway, no one will want me near them in case I infect them with my disease, and my friends say that wherever this man is he's followed by crowds of people. So, it's pointless even to consider their idea.

More importantly, I know I smell and the few clothes I have aren't fit to be seen. As to how my friends will get me there, well, that's another problem to be overcome.

I'm not going to allow them to take me out amongst our neighbours. That's bad enough, it would be much worse to be seen by people coming from other villages, and especially, by the Priests and Pharisees.

I can't bear it, it's bad enough knowing I'm a cripple, but my heart shrivels within me at the prospect of everyone looking at me in this state.

This is usually such a quiet village but today it's taken on a whole new look and sound. There's a terrible noise and commotion down at the house on the corner. I can just see people all crowding together. So many people, all blocking the street round the house, in fact the entire house looks as if it is full to bursting point. No wonder all those people are outside trying to get in. I suppose that's how I see myself as being outside of everything—a useless, helpless, cripple. That's me.

There are even Priests and Pharisees coming down the street, talking and discussing in their usual stuck up way. Huh! I've no time for them or for the fancy clothes they wear as they strut about looking important, when all they really are is useless. Well that's something they and I have in common anyway. Uselessness.

More and more of them arrive, Pharisees and teachers of the Law. They're even pushing our own villagers out of the way, so that they can get to the front of the crowd. They are so sure of themselves. I hate their self-satisfied attitude and I've yet to find them of any real use when we, the ordinary people, need help.

Of course this makes me wonder yet again what this man Jesus can possibly do for me. After all he is just an ordinary man from an ordinary background and probably wearing ordinary clothes. It's all so pointless even to think of allowing my friends to take me to see Jesus.

Four against one is a lost argument, so it becomes pointless to object as my friends hoist my bed up and tie it to a pole, so that they can carry me. Lifting, heaving and pushing, my friends carry me to the edge of the crowd. I bury my face in my hands. My flesh crawls with embarrassment and my nails tear at my scalp with the fear of being on show to everyone.

Amazingly the crowd are so fixed on getting near Jesus that they don't seem to notice us at all. "May the Lord be praised!" The crowd seems to have a power all of its own as we are shoved, pushed and jostled to the front of the house and then—I knew it would be useless. There's no way inside. Too many people.

I'm being thrown around all over the place on this bed. Now I'm being lifted up at an angle. This whole thing is terrible. I'm going to fall out and then everyone will see my shrivelled legs and my bent back. Worse still they are certain to smell my fear.

I have never known fear like this. Fear of being seen in this crippled state. Fear of this huge crowd and of the scorn that the Pharisees will heap upon me at the sight of this pathetic body. I'm even afraid of this Jesus and what he will do. And I think I'm even afraid of fear itself.

I do not believe it! We're on the roof and my friends are taking the roof apart. The owner will be furious.

Now I feel as if I'm falling over a cliff. They're lowering me down to the floor. All these faces staring, and the Priests and the Pharisees complaining and condemning loudly as I come to rest at their feet.

As I dare to lift myself onto my elbow and look, all I can see in front of me is the edge of a grubby, travel stained robe and two worn feet.

As I stare at this figure in front of me the warmth begins. It flows all over me and even into my gut. I've never known anything like it. I want to shout out the word "Love, Love, Love." This is amazing, just being in Jesus' presence is like being bathed in love, like I've never known in my life.

"Your sins are forgiven," Jesus' words seem to wash me with healing oil.

Yes, that's it. He knows all about me and the comfort of him knowing, is like oil pouring into my entire being, soothing away all the feelings of fear and uselessness. I am being forgiven, healed, restored, made new by HIM!

"Your sins are forgiven." Jesus' words are restoring my very soul. Yes, that's it he can save me, save me, even from myself.

"Your sins are forgiven." Love and acceptance burst from my gut and engulf me in a tide of grace, God's own grace.

I can hear Jesus telling the Pharisees that he knows they are thinking that he has no authority to forgive sins. Well I know in my soul that God has forgiven me and I am changed forever. I am no longer useless. What a miracle.

Then Jesus says to them, "Why do you question in your hearts? Which is easier: to say, Your sins are forgiven, or to say, Get up and walk?"

My, these Pharisees are angry, I can almost feel their anger as they glare at me with fury. You would think I was the cause of all this upset. As for the crowd, they are all talking at once, as if they are confused about Jesus forgiving my sins. Well I'm not confused. I've never felt so whole and accepted in my life.

Then Jesus said, "But that you may know that the Son of Man has authority on earth to forgive sins." And he turned to me , saying, "I tell you, get up, take your mat and go home." The power of those words is more than I can bear, they seem to be reaching into every part of my body and lifting me up, and up, and up. I'm standing, standing on my feet. My legs, my legs are strong and full. They're no longer shrivelled. My back's straight. Oh so straight.

I want to fall at Jesus' feet but I don't. I pick up my mat and begin to walk to my house in the sure and certain knowledge that I have already come home. You see, I have found my home in him—in Jesus.

The silence of the crowd is tangible for they too know they are in the presence of he who has authority on earth to forgive sins.

> Lord, in our weakness, be our strength.
>
> Lord, when we feel outcast and afraid, touch us with your acceptance.
>
> Lord, draw us to yourself, that we may find our home in you, now and forever.

The Issue

A large crowd followed and pressed around him. And a woman was there who had been subject to bleeding for twelve years. She had suffered a great deal under the care of many doctors and had spent all she had, yet instead of getting better she grew worse. When she heard about Jesus, she came up behind him in the crowd and touched his cloak, because she thought, "If I just touch his clothes, I will be healed." Immediately her bleeding stopped and she felt in her body that she was freed from her suffering. Mark 5:25-34

"Jesus is coming!" "Jesus is coming!" The cries echo from person to person. The crowd grows and swells in anticipation and excitement as they move along the road as one mass. That's me excluded from even going to catch a glimpse of him, never mind getting near to him.

This problem—no it's an issue—has dogged me for over 12 years, years of misery and exclusion. I'm considered unclean by the standards of Mosaic Law and therefore not welcome anywhere, not even in the Court of Women in the Temple.

I weep tears of pain and misery. Lord! Where are you in my desolation? You, who created women—to bear children. That's an amazing, wonderful privilege. But, the very root of my constant struggle is what you created in me. How can you allow my womanhood to be the very cause of my suffering like this? I just don't understand.

So, why am I interested in Jesus coming? What can he possibly do for me?

My husband avoids me. My sons don't really give me any love and my daughters live in fear that a similar fate will befall them too. How could you? You, who are Almighty God. As for all my neighbours, they treat me as if I were a leper. And all because I'm a woman, a woman with what amounts to a curse on her life.

Financially, I'm spent. All those doctors—and of course they are all men—men, who don't really understand my issue at all. Oh, they can hand out potions and charge a fortune, but none of the 'cures' ever work. So, I'm bereft of healing, money, friends and family.

Lord it is too much to bear. My body is screaming out against all the physical weakness. As for my spirit, it's struggling with the understanding of you as male. So, perhaps I shouldn't be expecting you to do anything about my problem.

So, what can this Jesus do for me? He's a man as well!

I've heard so much about him, how he helps and heals people, even women. In fact it's rumoured that there are women in his group of followers. Even so, there's no use me thinking about trying to meet him. He's a man and I'm a woman with an issue; an issue that's not only physical, it's emotional. I'm continually struggling with this raw wound of being a woman, and it doesn't stop there. There are the social struggles of being considered unclean and therefore not fit for company. As for the spiritual aspect of this whole thing, that's the hardest of all to bear. To feel so unclean that I can't come into the Synagogue to be near you Lord, you who made me. That's the biggest struggle of all, these Priests, Scribes and Pharisees treating me as if I am contaminated. Certainly, if they just brush against me, the Law demands that they have to wash immediately. Ritual washing cleanses and sets *them* free, but not me. I'm left in the same humiliating state as before.

To be so humiliated in life leaves me without hope, not quite despairing but nearly so. Yet, somehow these cries of, "Jesus is coming!" stir a frisson of hope deep within, and with it comes a vague expectation that he will be able to deal with my problem. I wonder what he would think if he knew I was taking issue with you Lord. Now I've nearly missed him in all this crush. It's my own fault! If I hadn't been so busy talking about my problems to you Lord, I wouldn't have been left behind.

That's odd. The crowd seems to have come to halt. I can just make out a man who looks very important. Why, it's Jairus, one of the rulers in the Synagogue and he's talking with Jesus. I wonder what he wants with him. It sounds like something to do with his daughter being sick and needing healing. My, that is an amazing thing to see. Jairus, asking this Jesus for help! Strange contrast here, Jairus, so well dressed and important on his knees before Jesus, who wears a simple robe and is clearly unimportant. Jairus, in a posture of begging—looks more like an act of worship to me.

Lord, your Law says, "Thou shalt have no other gods before me." So, what has made Jairus act like this? What on earth will people think? After all he does have his status to maintain. Even if his daughter is sick, for him to fall at the feet of Jesus is outrageous behaviour for a man of his importance.

Now if I could just reach Jesus and tell him about my problem, he might be willing to listen to me. Of course, he daren't touch me in my unclean state. But, if I could reach out and touch the hem of his garment, he wouldn't even know, especially in this crush.

That's it, nearly there! If I can just get a bit closer, that should do it. If he'd only move back a bit he would be within reach. I could stretch out my hand and touch the tip of his hem with my fingers.

As my fingers make contact with the hem of his coat I'm flooded with a warmth that reaches into every part of me. What a warmth, and with it comes a sensation of...I recognise this sensation, but it's a long lost experience from way back when I was younger and free to be in the Synagogue. I'm not quite sure what it is.

Then in a flash, it's there—the knowledge of his love, and joy and grace pouring into me! And all this from simply touching his garment. Overcome with the power of this love, I move away, so overwhelmed that I can scarcely stand. And, knowing in an instant—for that's all this took—knowing that my issues of body, mind and spirit are healed!

"Who touched my clothes?" Jesus asked. My heart lurches with fear and amazement as I hear him ask this question. How could he possibly know in such a crush that someone has touched him?

Here we go again, "Unclean woman!" Of course, he's a man isn't he?

He's searching the crowd now, looking to see who has touched him. As he turns in my direction I am compelled to move towards him and fall at his feet, pouring out everything to him. I'm amazed that he listens to it all. Even Jairus and the other men don't move away. I tell him that I knew if I could just touch the hem of his garment I would be healed, and how I had felt so unclean, unloved and worthless that nobody could possibly know my true worth. But, he did.

"Your faith has made you whole," he said. My faith! He knew all about me, all my struggles and issues with you Lord, and he still poured out his grace and healing right into my heart. That's it! That's the feeling I remember from my childhood days, the feeling of being loved and accepted by Almighty God as I worshipped in the Synagogue.

I'm being nourished with Jesus' love, and in my soul, I now know my true worth, as a woman, loved and created by God. As I stand before Jesus, it's as if the whole of eternity comes to meet me and wrap around me with the certainty of who this man Jesus really is—the King of Kings and Lord of Lords.

"Go in peace and be released from your suffering." (Mark 5:34)

> Lord, where I have issues, show me.
>
> Lord, help me to know that I can share all my issues with you.
>
> When the issues of life overwhelm my being, help me to reach out and touch the hem of your garment.
>
> Lord, help me to be a blessing to others, when they struggle with life's issues.

Jairus and his Daughter

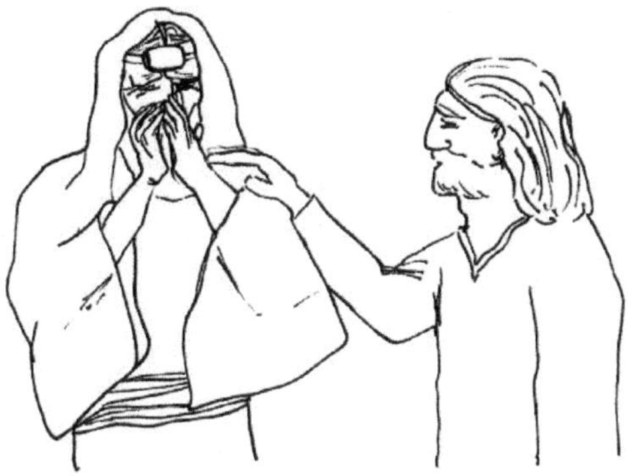

While Jesus was still speaking, someone came from the house of Jairus, the Synagogue ruler, "Your daughter is dead," he said. "Don't bother the teacher anymore."

Hearing this, Jesus said to Jairus, "Don't be afraid; just believe, and she will be healed." Luke 8:49-50

She's not moving! She can't be so ill that she doesn't know me, her own father. Oh! Lord! Lord! You've got to save her. She's only twelve years old. But of course, you know that already. I can't bear to see the distress of my wife. It's too much to endure.

What are we going to do? She's so listless and pale—like alabaster. Ah! The pain of helplessness is like a raw wound gnawing away at my gut. This feeling of desperation is completely new to me. I'm usually the one in control.

Desperate, yes, I'm desperate that you're not answering me Lord! Do you hear me? Or are you stuck inside your book of Holy Scriptures? Desperation is causing me to lose my reason, if anyone were to hear me—I'd be accused of blasphemy. Not good!

Help me! Help me! Lord. You have to help my daughter. Your word says."I will rescue him I will protect him." But right now, mere words are of no use to me. I need you! You! Yes, you yourself Lord! Not empty words on a page.

Jesus! The teacher from Nazareth, he's the answer! Well, maybe not, none of us leaders and Pharisees can really agree whether he is a genuinely godly man or an imposter. His teaching seems to cut to the heart of our religion in such a uniquely challenging way, as if highlighting all its restrictions, and yet, at the same time illuminating all the treasures of God. It's all strangely compelling.

The biggest problem lies with all the reports of the blind seeing, lepers being cleansed and the lame walking. Frightening stuff! We rulers have never been able to heal, so, how can an itinerant preacher from Nazareth of all places, do what we—the religious elite—can't? It seems to defy all your laws.

I can't be thinking like this. My mind and my feet seem to be tripping over each other in my haste to reach Jesus. It's as if I'm running through a black tunnel of fear and confusion; heading straight to despair.

There he is! He's got to listen, "Jesus! Jesus! Help me! My daughter of twelve is sick." My heart feels as if it's being torn open with the pain of it all, and worse still I'm on the ground at *His* feet, as if in worship! This is humility. Do you realise Lord that I've given up my status to grovel in the dirt in front of an itinerant preacher, and all because you didn't take the time to answer me!

Mind you, anything for my daughter! Anything at all!

Dead! Dead? They're saying she's dead, she can't be. She's only twelve. She's hardly lived. I knew you weren't even listening to me Lord. It's so cold and black, in this tunnel of despair and fear. The coldness of her death seems to be gripping my every breath. My life is finished! Dead!

"Don't be afraid; just believe, and she will be healed." The sound, the very sound of his voice is pushing the darkness back giving me the strength to stand on my feet to go to my daughter.

I almost give up as the eerie wails of the neighbours hit my ears, sending cold shivers of dread into the depths of my being. "Don't be afraid, don't be afraid." The words, but more importantly, the absolute power in his voice, cause a glimmer of hope to warm my heart. That hope is like a river of power pouring into me. Now there is hope. Real hope, in place of despair.

She's dead, dead, dead! My thoughts seem to echo the wails of the woman. They are just like wild dogs waiting to devour their prey. The confusion is blighting my thinking. If I were fit to think coherently, I would not even allow this hope to surface at all. Oh my daughter! My daughter!

"Don't be afraid." Maybe he's right and she won't die. Maybe, just maybe, Jesus is right after all. Just being near him brings a confidence and a strange sense of comfort deep down.

"Don't be afraid; just believe, and she will be healed." As we stare at her lying there so still and quiet, Jesus' voice penetrates the silence with a power beyond my imagining. "My child, get up!" She's standing up! She's healed! The black tunnel of despair and hopelessness is flooding with the light of you Lord. You have heard me.

Not only have you heard my plea, you have come to my rescue. In Person.

"Don't be afraid," Now I am secure in the comfort of your power.

"Don't be afraid," My courage is renewed in your presence.

"Don't be afraid," My soul is illuminated by the light of your love.

I only needed to remain in your presence to witness the hope in my heart becoming real before me

"Don't be afraid." "Don't be afraid."

> Lord, when fears overwhelm us, touch us with your comfort.
>
> Lord, when life demands more from us than we are able to cope with, fill us with your presence.
>
> Lord, when life becomes dark around us, fill us with the light and warmth of your love.

Lord, when the light of your love finds its home in our hearts, help us to share that love with others.

Thank You

One of them, when he saw he was healed, came back, praising God in a loud voice. He threw himself at Jesus' feet and thanked him—and he was a Samaritan.

Luke17:11-19

The dampness of the cave seems to be more penetrating than ever today and my bones feel as if they are being gnawed at by the dankness of this hell we're all forced to live in.

Live! Well, I'd hardly call this living at all. Existing more like! Merely existing; grasping at anything that seems remotely normal: a breath of fresh air, a glimpse of the sun, a scraping of food; and we all think we've been given a precious gift. Which of course we have!

Sun and air on our faces lift away the sense of living under the curse of death, which feels as if it's reaching out to overwhelm us and reduce us to even less than we know in our hearts that we are.

The darkness of this disease seems to devour our very humanity, reducing us to mere creatures. No! I won't voice the word 'animals', because we're not. We're not! We're never that! We have to find a way of holding onto our humanity. I suppose every little thing we do for each other keeps us human, even sane. It would be easy, oh so easy, to allow ourselves to wallow in despair.

The stink in this place is foul, really foul. But we're fortunate that we're only twenty in number—not like some of the other caves and hideouts with more than thirty lepers in each.

My sores are getting worse and I've no feeling at all in my toes or feet. Humph! I've plenty of feeling in my heart—furious, burning, blazing anger and resentment at being reduced to a stinking rag-clad wretch.

This contrast of feelings is too much to cope with—no physical feeling where I need it in my feet and my toes, and yet I have these all-consuming feelings where I don't need them or even want them.

Help me, Lord! Oh help me Lord! I don't understand how you can allow us, to suffer all this degradation.

There might just be a glimmer of hope for us. There have been rumours about a man called Jesus, who they claim heals the sick and even lepers like us. I'm really struggling to believe this far-fetched story. After all, lepers are lepers. It's always been thus—no acceptance; treated with suspicion; excluded from society for fear of touching someone; and certainly no cure. How can this Jesus even come near us—near enough to touch us and heal us?

Ten of us are going to see if all the stories about Jesus are true; that he's not afraid to touch lepers and he might even heal us. Ten of us together. Safety in numbers. And, we can support each other on the way.

My heart is hammering in my chest with the fear of 'What if?' What if we trust and believe that Jesus will heal us, and he refuses? What if we are healed? I could go back home again. This is like being on the edge of a chasm and looking out on an empty space. Will I be able to live with myself as the new me, if I am healed?

As the ten of us draw near to the town we can see Jesus with his friends, but by law we're forbidden from approaching him.

The sweat of fear is trickling down my face and dripping off the end of my nose. As for the others, they're shaking as if they are about to die. Will he? Won't he? He won't even look at us! We're just like rubbish! Maybe we should just give up now.

The babble of our doubts and fears seems to be filling the distance between him and us and strangely gives us the courage to call out to him. "Jesus, Master, have pity on us!"

"Go, show yourselves to the priests." That is all, "Go, show yourselves to the priests." That is all it takes, and yet it is more than enough. We all feel the warmth of acceptance. It is more than that, our cold, empty, pitiful bodies feel as if they're filling with the most amazing sense of love any of us has ever known.

We turn as one, to do as Jesus commands. And, then it begins.

One after another the miracle touches each one of us. Dirty stinking flesh becomes clean and fresh! Faces eaten away over the months and years into unspeakable horror are restored to the fullness of wholeness and beauty.

We stare at each other in awe and wonder, as we behold this amazing miracle happening to each one of us. Tears flow unchecked as we realize the gift we've been given. Now we're all dancing, shouting and singing with joy—joy like a river rushing through us in torrents.

My feet are whole! My hands are complete! Who is this man Jesus? He's healed without touch. We're healed simply by the sound of his voice. Healed, I can't take it in, and my tears are now tears of gratitude.

My heart and my very soul, feel as if they are being filled with love, joy, peace and hope all at once. Thank you Lord! Thank you!

I *have* to go back and thank Jesus. He has given me a gift beyond price. Even my soul feels healed and cleansed. I am made new! His voice is like an echo in my soul drawing me back to him. I *have* to go back and say, "Thank you!"

Approaching him, I am completely overcome with his power and fall at his feet in gratitude.

"Were not all ten cleansed? Where are the other nine? Was no one found to return and give praise to God except this foreigner?" Then he said, "Rise and go; your faith has made you well."

His voice fills me again, this time with a peace beyond my understanding and strangely I don't feel like a mere Samaritan in his presence. I know I belong to him.

He has to be the Messiah!

> Lord, when we feel outcast and afraid, touch us with your presence.
>
> Lord, when life overwhelms us, shield us with your love.
>
> Lord, when we feel less than whole, help us to hear your healing words.
>
> Lord, help us to accept your gift of healing in our lives.

By Night

Now there was a man of the Pharisees named Nicodemus, a member of the Jewish ruling council. He came to Jesus at night and said, "Rabbi, we know you are a teacher who has come from God. For no-one could perform the miraculous signs you are doing if God were not with him."

In reply, Jesus declared, "I tell you the truth, no-one can see the kingdom of God unless he is born again."

"How can a man be born when he is old?" Nicodemus asked. "Surely he cannot enter a second time into his mother's womb to be born!"

In reply Jesus declared, "I tell you the truth no-one can enter the kingdom of God unless he is born of water and the Spirit. Flesh gives birth to flesh, but the Spirit gives birth to Spirit. You should not be surprised at my saying, 'You must be born again.'" John 3:1-8

My own authority was not in question. But, it seemed almost impossible to bring this particular discussion to a conclusion, especially since it concerned this new teacher Jesus and his ideas—ideas that are more than challenging to our understanding of the Law.

The arguments and discussions went on and on and on as if forever—the Sanhedrin at their worst. Everyone disputing points of the Law, until the conversation became so convoluted that no one seemed to remember the original point of it all.

Of course our problems as Pharisees are two-fold. One is status—what we are in the eyes of the community, the learned, the leaders, the elite. Secondly, and perhaps more importantly—how we perceive ourselves in relation to each other and our personal wealth.

Wealth and power—two very demanding 'masters'. I sometimes think that we each allow them to dominate our thinking and undermine our faith and confidence in the Lord until *they* take first place in our lives. So much for, "Thou shalt have no other god's before me."

We are so moulded by the teaching of the prophets and the Law of Moses that it feels almost blasphemous to allow myself to even think in a different way. However, the real issue for me is that, as a Pharisee and a ruler, I must not allow anyone to even suspect that I am being challenged by Jesus' teaching.

You see, his teaching seems to go so much deeper than mere statements and points of Law. And, yes, Jesus does make the fundamentals of my faith seem less important in one way; but so much more important in another.

He is so simple and yet compelling, both in his presence and in his teaching. It's as if he stirs my very soul with the presence of God himself! My thinking in this way will be considered blasphemous by some of the Sanhedrin. Indeed, for a Pharisee, a ruler and a teacher of the Law and the Prophets, these are very dangerous thoughts to have.

Perhaps if I seek him out at night I will be safe from prying eyes and wagging tongues and then my integrity will remain intact.

This feeling of fear is completely irrational. It's not simply to do with status. It goes much deeper than that, penetrating to the core of my faith as I have known it since childhood. The thought of meeting with Jesus is a threat to my innermost being. I will have to spread out before him, like a carpet, all I have ever believed and known in my mind and more importantly in my intellect.

What a strange and unsettling thought to have. My commonsense tells me that he will not be able to see what I don't want him to see. And of course, someone like Jesus can't possibly understand someone like me. Or, there again, can he?

The darkness is almost overwhelming me, as if reaching into my being to hold me back from this meeting. Yet, I have a sense of being drawn through the darkness, as if towards the light.

Then suddenly, we are face to face. And, as if, pouring out from a tiny spot of light in the distance, all light and truth are incarnate in him; flooding into my mind, my will and even my emotions. All this in Jesus and his words, "You must be born again". He is the source of this light! He is the light!

As I look at him, he radiates every little facet of God as I have ever understood him. But more! Much more! Now I am conscious as never before of areas of my life I have never allowed myself to consider. "You must be born again". I'm suddenly sure of my next move, I have to lay at his feet all of my life, give him my very heart and of course my mind. That's a hard one. That will be like giving him all I possess.

After all, my mind is unique, and of course it gives me control over everything I do and say, and my enjoyment of the way I think. It is my treasure above all else.

Fear digs at the pit of my stomach. Apprehension is tying me up, as if the very phylacteries on my forehead and my hand have become fetters, holding me in a place of darkness. My confusion grows as I become more and more aware of this light, warm and comforting, wrapping me in an acceptance that is beyond my understanding.

I have served God and the Scriptures all my life. But, to serve God and to serve the Scriptures is not the same thing. I have created God in my image and my thinking—a god of laws and rituals, office and observance. And that only requires outward acts, where I don't have to feel, or give of my heart.

This is what Jesus means about being "born again". I have to give him my heart, and my mind. As his love penetrates to my very soul, my resistance melts in the warmth of his love. I silently give God my mind, my will, and indeed, my soul. And I lay my life at his feet as an offering.

YES! That's it! He is the Law and the Scriptures and the Prophets. He is God with us!

The darkness of the night is gone. Only the light of eternal truth remains. And, I am born again, in Him.

> Lord, where we struggle to hold onto our treasure, show us your treasure.
>
> Where we lock our hearts tight in our ideas, touch our hearts with the freedom of your truth.
>
> Where we struggle with your word, enlighten our minds with your wisdom.
>
> Where we resist your Holy Spirit, fill us with your presence, bringing your new birth to our very souls, so that we might be born again, day after day.

Changed

When Jesus reached the spot, he looked up and said to him, 'Zacchaeus, come down immediately. I must stay at your house today.' So he came down at once and welcomed him gladly. Luke 19: 5-6

That's all the money counted for the last two days so it needs to be kept safely until collection day. Not a bad skim, probably about ten Denarii for myself which means I can afford to have all the extras I want in the way of clothes and the new bed mats I've craved for so long.

I suppose I did feel a pang of guilt at taking that extra Denarius from Anna. She is a widow after all. But then again, I've got to live, and my need is just as great as hers. At least, I think it is!

Well, maybe not! The thing is, if I don't skim, where am I? The Romans do not pay well, so all the little 'extras' ease my life nicely.

Of course the people hate me. No-one speaks, and I'm always ignored. I've even been spat on and reviled, so the extra money is at least some compensation for their hatred and ridicule of me.

The word is that Jesus of Nazareth is coming our way and I would really like to see him. But, and it's a big but, my short legs won't allow me to see over the heads of the people. There's sure to be crowds and crowds of them all coming to see, and more importantly, to hear Jesus speak.

I've heard all the talk about how Jesus teaches with an insight that is life changing. It's said that he heals the sick, makes the blind see and that even the lame are cured by him. I'm not sure about the life changing aspect of Jesus' teaching, because if I go to see him I might just be influenced towards change.

No! No! Not change that's more than I can bear to consider. This is not good! I feel scared, threatened even, and I only ever feel threatened when I think there might be a problem collecting the taxes. I suppose my biggest fear is when I'm faced with people who are taller than me, especially if it happens to be a woman!

These feelings of fear and anxiety are ridiculous. I am a man of financial substance, nice house, fine clothes, plenty of good food and of course servants. Mind you, no friends; and that can be a bit lonely. Still, having plenty of money means I can at least be miserable in comfort!

Furthermore, my wealth gives me stature, even providing me with a kind of height. It raises me above everyone else. My wealth is my all, elevating me to a place of power and authority over all these lesser mortals. So, change is impossible for me to consider. It would mean losing too much. However, I can still go to see Jesus, but I don't have to listen to him.

After all my wealth is my strength, and of course my insurance against all change, and my protection against adversity.

My wealth has certainly proven its worth. If I'm spat upon I'm able to treat that with disdain, because I am so much richer than the person spitting at me.

If I'm shunned by my neighbours, I simply take comfort in thinking about all my wealth.

If I feel lonely I admire my fine house and all my valuable treasures.

If I suffer a pang of guilt at being so well off, that's easily enough dealt with. I just throw some coins at the beggars in the street. Just a few coins mind you, because being so poor they've no status to maintain and that immediately assuages any pangs of guilt I might be feeling.

Yes! Yes! To have money is most definitely the answer to all the problems of life. There's absolutely no doubt about that at all.

I need to stop thinking and debating with myself. I must try to get past all these people! What a crush! The entire village seems to be here and they're nearly all taller and heavier than I am—even the women! If I could just use some of my money to pay them to stand back, so that I could get to the front, I would have a better chance of seeing Jesus.

No one is likely to accept anything from me. Huh! This is the first time I've not been able to use my wealth to get what I want. I really do not like this not being in control.

I don't stand a chance of getting a sight of Jesus. Unless? Unless I can climb up this tree! I would have a terrific view of everything and I would be up above everyone else.

I was right! Being up this tree is the answer, apart from tearing my robe on that big branch. Now I can watch everything. And, more important, Jesus won't know I'm here.

Here he comes, surrounded by his friends and followers. Huh! Not one of them looks worth much, in fact they're a poor looking bunch.

Oh! He's stopped right underneath me and he's talking and laughing; laughing and talking with all the people, none of them really wealthy or important, and here am I stuck up a tree!

What on earth am I doing up this tree? It's a real change for me not to be in the very best position to meet Jesus.

My heart is thudding in my chest and my mind feels as if it's chasing round and round in circles—just like coins all rolling about when they're dropped.

This is not good. I feel ill, sick, overwhelmed, as if by a great wind, pushing and blowing my mind and emotions into a terrible confusion of thoughts and feelings. I feel as if my wealth is like a band round my head, becoming tighter and tighter. I can't stand this! It's as if I'm in the grip of some kind of change, change that's turning my very soul inside out!

Worse upon worse! Jesus lifts his head and looks directly at me with love filled eyes; eyes that pierce the core of my being with an all-pervading warmth, and a power that looks into and beyond my very soul.

My wealth is as nothing compared to this man!

Now my mind is flooding with images, images of all the people I've cheated. They're all there, mirrored in his gaze. I feel as if I'm being emptied out like a bag of worthless coins about to be counted and I can't even draw my gaze away from his.

I want all this to stop now! But, it doesn't stop! Instead, feelings of sorrow and regret engulf my being.

And, still he holds my gaze. His gaze (for no word has been spoken) releases in me a compelling urge to shout to the crowd, "I'm sorry, so very sorry for all the wrongs I've done you, all the money I've stolen, yes, stolen from you!"

I don't even have to hear his voice. I only have to look at him to know that he is changing my heart. Such a change! I was blinded and weighed down with wealth. Now, I see with the eyes of my heart. It's as if he's breathing new life into my soul.

His very presence is turning me inside out—I need to make amends for all my cheating. I want more than anything to restore to the people their dignity and worth, by repaying them. My shame is consuming me with fear and regret—regret at having lost my soul to money—and my honour as a good Israelite, by selling myself to the Romans to do their work for them.

My mind seems to whisper the words, "Lord, change me! Change even me!"

"Zacchaeus, come down immediately. I must stay at your house today." The sound of his voice filled me with an excitement that seemed to flow into and all over me. And, as I come down from the tree, I know that I am free, free to say to Jesus, "Lord! Here and now I give half of my possessions to the poor and if I have cheated anybody out of anything I will pay back four times the amount."

As I uttered these words, my wealth seemed to become a cascade of coins falling to the ground;

becoming as it fell, nothing more than worthless rubbish, blowing away in the wind.

My treasure is in him who called me down from the tree, and my riches are in him. My heart is his. My stature is assured, now and forever. Then he crowns my joy with the words, "Today Salvation has come to this house, because this man too is a son of Abraham. For, the Son of Man came to seek and to save the lost."

I am changed indeed! Now I see!

Lord, when we struggle with the power of money, turn us to you.

Lord, when our sight is dazzled by the false brightness of wealth, shine your true light into our hearts.

Lord, when we imagine that our status and stature depend on our possessions, show us the cross of Jesus.

Lord, keep showing us by the power of your spirit that our true wealth lies in you.

An environmentally friendly book printed and bound in England by www.printondemand-worldwide.com

PEFC Certified

This product is from sustainably managed forests and controlled sources

www.pefc.org

PEFC/16-33-415

This book is made of chain-of-custody materials; FSC materials for the cover and PEFC materials for the text pages.